Job Interview Prep Book for Men, Women and Teens

Answer the Tough Questions and handle Your Interview with Confidence and Ease!

By Brian Mahoney

Disclaimer Notice

This book was written as a guide and for information, educational and entertainment purposes only. No warranties of any kind are expressed or implied.

Readers acknowledge that the author is not engaging in the rendering of legal, financial, medical or professional advice, and the information in this book is not meant to take the place of any professional advice. If advice is needed in any of these fields, you are advised to seek the services of a professional.

While the author has attempted to make the information in this book as accurate as possible, no guarantee is given as to the accuracy or currency of any individual item. Laws and procedures related to business, health and well being are constantly changing.

Therefore, in no event shall the author of this book be liable for any special, indirect, or consequential damages or any damages whatsoever in connection with the use of the information herein provided.

TABLE OF CONTENTS

The author been interviewed and hired by...

* Four Star Restaurants

* The Unites States Army

* The United States Postal Service

* Meijer's

* Walt Disney World

and run 7 successful business's.

RESPONSIBILITY (noun)

re·spon·si·bil·i·ty | \ ri-ˌspän(t)-sə-ˈbi-lə-tē \

plural responsibilities

Definition of responsibility

1 : the quality or state of being responsible: such as

a : moral, legal, or mental accountability

b : reliability, trustworthiness

"Employers want to higher someone who projects they are responsible."

...Brian Mahoney

Introduction

"An investment in knowledge pays the best interest."

Benjamin Franklin

Are you looking for your next ample opportunity and want to land the job of your dreams? Have you recently graduated from high school or college and are looking to get a job in your field? Do you have a strong resume but don't know how to enhance your interview repertoire?

If you answered yes to any of those questions, then this is the perfect book for you. You may be going through a transition and have decided to change your field of interest, or perhaps you have held a job for several years, and you need to brush up on your interview skills to land another interview and get the job that you've worked hard for. In any of these cases, it is essential to develop strong skills for interviewing.

These days, more people are moving from job to job within a short period. Sometimes, people change jobs every two years; others may stay in the same position for at least three years. The truth is that most people will move to another job at least a few times throughout their careers.

Gone are the days when you could be loyal to a company and guaranteed job security for life. This is no longer the case. Most of the time with millennials, who are currently the generation developing in the workforce, people are moving on to different jobs at least once every three years.

The reasons for this can include gaining better working conditions, an increased salary, a better work-life balance, or better compatibility with the person's values.

Millennials, in particular, want to make a difference in the world, and they see their job as a platform to change society. This is unique from previous generations, though it is something that most generations have been working towards.

With people changing jobs over short periods, they need to develop their interview skills. It is not easy to interview, but it is an important life skill. Just because you have landed an excellent job and see yourself staying there for a while doesn't mean you should become complacent and forget about the basics of interviewing.

You may think that just because you have a connection with someone in the company, you are automatically in and can get whatever job you want; that certainly is not the case. You have to work hard at preparing for interviews and developing your skills to get a job easily. That takes time and dedication, which you will need to commit to it.

Job interview preparation can often become a full-time job, especially in today's competitive work environment, where there are fewer jobs for highly skilled workers who are well-educated and have experience. Many people don't tell you this, but many workers are out of work and looking for work in their field but are spending months or even upwards of a year or two trying to get a job. This is one of the sad realities of today's world, and it is not an easy thing to deal with. This is why it is necessary to know how to prepare for an interview.

During my forty-plus years of experience as a member of management or as a consultant, I hired or was part of the team that hired hundreds of employees.

Given that I hired hundreds of employees, I estimate that I interviewed more than 1,000 candidates over forty years. As someone doing the hiring, I can assure you that the one thing that impacts a candidate getting hired is the interview.

This book is a guide that will help you prepare for your next interview. We will provide you with detailed information about preparing for the interview, what to do during the interview, and how to act after the interview.

There are important steps and tips that will help you get through every part of the process. Sometimes, you have to work strategically because you never know how many applicants are applying for your job or how much you need to stand out from the crowd.

What's important is that you are well-prepared to make an impression because first impressions count the most. You have only one opportunity to impress the interviewer.

Do you want to blow your chances or charm your interviewer? That's where this book comes in - to help you blow your interviewer away with your wit, skill, expertise, and attitude.

It all starts with proving that you are qualified for the position and that you will work well with the organization, including your interpersonal skills. Making this impression is an important part of the process, and you have to play your cards well. That means paying attention to the small details because those will be important as you begin this process.

Focus your attention on how you can prepare. Come along with us on this journey to discover how to prepare yourself for the interview. You will not be disappointed; we guarantee that these tips will be helpful as you prepare for your next career move.

With a little knowledge and practice, you can craft a cover letter that will get you noticed, write a resume that will draw attention to your strengths, conduct an interview that illustrated how you are the perfect fit for the job, and follow up to the interview confidently to increase your chances of success.

Within the pages of this book, you will find all the information you need to succeed. All that is required is to put in the time, effort, and hard work to attain your dreams.
Happy reading!

Chapter 1:

Job Interviews

Applying for a job is often a very lengthy process.

From sending in your cover letter and resume to going in and sitting down for a face-to-face interview, the process can sometimes take up to several months. And while every step is essential, there is one step that is perhaps the most important: the interview.

The concept behind an interview is simple: In its simplest form, it is just a conversation or interaction between a person looking for a job and a person looking to hire someone for a job.

But an interview is so much more than a simple conversation between two people. An interview provides an opportunity for the candidate to meet and impress his potential employer. Moreover, it often determines whether or not the applicant will be offered the job.

An interview is useful for both the employer and the candidate. For the employer, it is a chance to meet the candidate and determine if he is a good fit for the position. For the candidate, it is an opportunity to observe the work environment and decide if the job is what he is looking for.

The Purpose of an Interview

There are four chief purposes of an interview.

1. An interview gives the employer a chance to meet the prospective employee and discuss his qualifications and experience level. It allows the employer to decide if the candidate is the best person for the job.
2. It allows the person seeking a job to learn more

about the company and the position he is interested in. He can learn more about the position and discuss why he is the best fit for the job with the employer.

3. It serves as a tool for screening candidates for forthcoming interviews.

4. It functions as a point where hiring decisions are made.

The Phases of an Interview

The interviewing process can be pretty intimidating if you are not familiar with the process. While most interviews differ from each other in certain aspects, they all involve the following three phases.

Before an Interview

Preparation is vital for all important tasks, and an interview is no exception. It is essential to prepare for the interview if you want to be hired. Many people, however, often overlook this and fail to achieve their goals. You can follow these tips to make sure you are as prepared as possible.

Know yourself:

Consider how well your skills, interests, values, experience, and education match the type of position and organization you are interviewing with.

Know the employer:

Research and find out all the details about the organization, the position, and the interviewer. Familiarize yourself with the organization's work, the salary range, the job position, and the workplace conditions.

You should know the mission and goals of the firm and the title and full name of the interviewer. All of this will enable you to ask well-informed questions during the interview.

There are plenty of resources to help you with this research. You can use the literature published by employers, such as annual reports, fact sheets, and brochures. You can also visit their website to find a description of their organizations and a list of job opportunities.

Gathering all of this information will not only help you prepare for the interview; it will also help reduce your anxiety.

Present a clean appearance:

Make sure that you sleep well the night before the interview. See to it that your appearance is neat and clean on the day of the interview. Your hair should be neat, nails and teeth should be clean, and your breath must be fresh. There should be no wrinkles on your clothes, and your shoes should be polished. Avoid wearing bold colors, short skirts, deep-cut blouses, noisy jewelry, strong cologne, and heavy makeup.

Arrive on time: Punctuality is essential. Make it a point to find out the exact location and time of the interview. Decide the route you will take beforehand and know how much time it will take to reach the destination.

To ensure you do not get lost, you can practice going to the location a few days before the scheduled interview. If you take public transportation, you should still practice going there a few days before.

Arrive at least 15 minutes before the interview. This will give you enough time to freshen up before meeting the interviewer.

Other things to keep in mind:

You should always go alone to interviews. Do not take children, spouses, or friends with you. Carry a notepad and a couple of ink pens or pencils. Keep some money for lunch and parking. Be sure to bring copies of reference letters, military records, your resume, and a form of identification.

During an Interview

An interview usually lasts 45 minutes, but it can be shorter or longer. Most interviews include an opening or greeting, followed by small talk, questions and answers, and then closing.

Opening or greeting:

A typical interview begins even before you enter the room. Therefore, it is necessary to be courteous and pleasant to anyone you meet.

Remember to be relaxed when you are waiting for the interviewer to come to meet you. Take some time to go through your resume and review your notes.

Take a look at the company's literature. Do not smoke, chew gum, slouch in the seat, or fidget with your clothes, tie, hair, nails, or lipstick.

Small talk:

You are evaluated as soon as you meet the interviewer. When you are introduced to the interviewer, it is expected that you shake hands with him. Do not hesitate to be the first one to put your hand forward. This will display your assertiveness.

You must refer to your interviewer by his name, smile at him, and greet him. For example, you can say, "Hello Mr. James, I am David Smith." At this juncture, you will face the interviewer directly and notice your dress and posture. He may notice if you are nervous or have some annoying mannerisms, so try to remain calm. Clasp your hands in front of you to keep yourself from fidgeting.

Keep standing until you are asked to take a seat and told where to hang your coat. Maintain a straight posture while sitting, and keep your feet steadily on the ground. Do not shake your leg or constantly move your feet because it will make you appear nervous. Try your best to maintain a confident appearance. Keep your notepad with you and put any other things on the ground beside your chair.

Most interviewers start the interview by talking about some general topics like weather or sports. Although these have nothing to do with your skills, you are evaluated at that time, too.

Interviewers assess your ability to communicate informally. Therefore, it is necessary to respond verbally instead of just a nod and a smile. Remember: This needs to be a conversation. Don't sit silently while the interviewer makes small talk.

IT SHOW TIME!

Question and answer:

The main portion of the interview begins when the interviewer starts to discuss the organization. You need to be ready to answer and maintain a conversation for nearly 15 to 30 minutes while he asks questions about your qualifications. The interviewer leads the conversation; therefore, you should pay attention to what is said and give a brief and precise answer.

Your answers should be related to the job and your skills. You can mention some examples from your past work. Speak in proper English and stay away from using slang. Try not to use fillers such as "you know," "uh," "um," or "like." Your speech should be clear, so do not mumble. Do not speak too fast or too slow.

Be ready with some questions to ask the interviewer after he has asked you questions. Make sure you ask questions that will elicit a positive response from your employer and show your knowledge of and interest in the position.

Do not shy away from asking questions. Asking questions shows you paid attention during the first part of the interview. Your well-informed queries will impress the employer and show that you are sincerely interested in the organization.

Closing:

The concluding part lasts for about five minutes but is still very important. During this time, the interviewer assesses your entire performance.

Continue to be courteous and enthusiastic. You can tell that the interview ends when the interviewer rustles the papers, glances at his watch, packs his belongings, stands, or says that he has gotten all of the required details.

When you notice such behavior, once again express your keenness for the job, stand up, shake hands with the interviewer, and thank him for his time and the opportunity to interview for the position. Smile and say goodbye. Remain confident and polite until you are out of sight.

After an Interview

Do not be under the impression that the interview ends when you leave the office. The follow-up process still has to be completed. Thank the interviewer by sending a thank you card, note, or email.

You can also call him on the phone to thank him. This will show your genuine interest in the job.
You can evaluate your experience after the interview.

Review your notes and think about what you could have done differently. Which area could you improve upon? Were there any questions you struggled to answer? What is your impression of the organization? What do you expect to happen next? Are you still interested in the job?

The Types of Job Interviews

Many employers conduct several interviews before offering the job to someone. This allows them to make sure they have selected the best candidate. Some common forms of interviews are explained below.

Telephonic Interview

A telephonic interview is typically a screening interview where the recruiter analyzes whether you can attend the second round of interviews. Although you are not directly meeting the recruiters, it doesn't mean that you can handle telephonic interviews without proper preparations. You have to invest time and effort to crack the telephonic interview.

Skype Interview

Skype video interviews have taken the world of telephonic interviews to the next level; in fact, most multinational companies prefer an initial Skype interview before conducting the usual one-on-one session with the candidates. This has made it easier for the recruiters to screen the candidates according to their ability to present themselves.

Skype interviews are also useful when the candidate is from a far-off location and cannot travel for the first round of an interview.

One on One Interview

One on One interviews are also sometimes referred to as traditional interviews. The format is like this: you will sit down with an interviewer who will ask you several questions designed to help the recruiter decide if you fit the job requirements. Although this format of interviewing sounds simple, it can get pretty tough.

Group Interview

Group interview is the opposite of panel interviews; one interviewer will interview several candidates at once. Group interviews are used for hiring certain positions, and the purpose of group interviews is to shortlist candidates from a group of several candidates. One of the most challenging parts of a group interview is to ensure that you stand out from the rest of the candidates. Although company's use group interviews to expedite the interview process, it might come as a rude shock to any candidate.

Summary

This chapter has outlined the various types of interviews as well as the three main interview stages. This chapter shed some light on how to present yourself before, during, and after your interview. The next chapter will show you how to answer some of the frequently asked questions in job interviews.

Chapter 2:

Toughest Interview Questions and the Best Answers

No two job interviews are the same. But job interviews generally follow a similar pattern with similar questions. You need to arm yourself with the kind of questions you should expect and the best response for each question.

Recruiters are also aware that there are many blogs with the title "How to Answer Job Interview Questions," and they can tell when you are merely reciting what you have memorized from another source. In other words, this is a guide on how to answer the questions and not precisely how you should answer the questions. I am giving you a pattern and some strategies. You should tailor them to fit your personal experiences.

Here are some of the most common job interview questions and how to answer them:

Tell Us About Yourself:

This is usually the first question, and practically all job interviewers ask it. You should expect it and prepare for it beforehand. It is, however, not an invitation for you to summarize your resume; they have seen your resume already and still want to know more about you.

It would be best if you talked about your background, and by background, I do not mean your family background and personal life history. Don't mention your marital status or any other personal matters, including religious or political views.

No matter how beautiful your family story may be, do not share it because that is not what they want to hear. Summarize your educational history in no more than three sentences, and talk about your professional experience if you have any. This is the time to clarify the gaps on your resume, if you have any.

Talk about your skills related to the position, and say a thing or two about your personality. All these should be in line with the role you are being interviewed for. And you should stop talking if you are cut short while you are still answering.

Why are you interested in working for us?

Sample answers:

1. I feel like it would be a privilege to work for a company with such a long-standing reputation. I researched your products and saw that you are considered one of the finest companies in the industry. The future prospects for the company are also promising and impressive. I will be proud to work as a member of your XYZ team. My background and skills fit this position perfectly.

2. Your firm won an award for making the excellent XYZ product that has helped countless people to improve their quality of life. That type of work is where I can put my skills to work in the best possible way. I was very excited when I saw this job opening. I know that your firm aims to provide excellent service. I also believe in the same values as your company. I feel that I can be a good member of your team.

Why should you be hired?

Sample answers:

1. I have been working as the assistant manager of XYZ Company for the past six years. I have acquired some solid motivational skills during this time. My methodologies for encouraging the employees to face challenges and meet deadlines have gained recognition, and I was given an award for my managerial skills last year. If I am hired, I can use these excellent strategies and leadership qualities to benefit this company.

2. My work experience and skills are a perfect match for this job. I possess excellent analytical skills and the ability to solve problems. I have successfully used these skills in my previous jobs and gained plenty of practical experience. I am a dedicated worker and have high standards of work. So if I am hired, I can be an asset to your company.

Can you tell us your strengths?

One of the most common interview questions has to do with strengths.   The question could be phrased in different ways.

Here are a few examples:

"What are your greatest strengths?"

"Name three things you do well?"

"What makes you think you are suited for this job?"

All these questions are designed to get you to talk about what you think you are good at. There are three rules in answering these types of questions.

Rule #1:

Your strengths should relate to the job. So, if the job is looking for someone with attention to detail, then attention to detail should be one of your strengths. Go back and look at the job ad, so you know what the company is looking for in a successful candidate. (Sidebar: Many candidates fail to read the job ads. Before the interview, read the job ad and highlight the important things that the employer is looking for.)

Rule #2:

You should have a demonstration to demonstrate your strength. So, if attention to detail was your strength, you need to talk about something you did that required great attention to detail (and at which you hopefully achieved success).

Rule #3:

Your strengths should all be character traits unless the job requires some particular and unique skills. Remember, an employer can teach skills but not character traits.

Can you tell us your weaknesses?

In addition to asking about strengths, an interviewer will most likely ask about weaknesses.   Again, like the strengths question, the actual question may be worded differently.

Here are some examples:

"Tell me about your greatest weaknesses?"

"Name three things you could improve on?"

"Where do you think you would find this job challenging?"

All these questions are designed to tell the interviewer about where you have problems and issues.

So how do you answer this question?

You start by denying that you have any weaknesses, specifically as it relates to the job.   Remember, you have a copy of the job ad.   When asked this question, take the copy of the job ad out of the folder on your lap, quickly read through the ad, and then respond something like this:

"Well, your ad says you are looking for someone who can work independently, someone who is detail-oriented, and someone who is a good communicator.

The person you are looking for is me.   I don't see that I have any weaknesses that would keep me from doing an excellent job for you."

Now, some interviewers may give you a pass and move on to the next question. However, experienced interviewers may press you by saying something like, "Oh, come on. Everyone has a weakness or needs to improve on something."

I like to answer this question with a joke, but not everyone is comfortable doing so. You must make sure your response fits your style. But if you use a joke, you could say something like,

"Well, my wife thinks I'm not doing a good job in taking out the garbage, so I guess I could improve on that." Even if you come back with a joke, you will need to talk about weaknesses once you get a laugh (assuming the interviewer has a sense of humor). You have no choice. You must answer. When you do answer, there are three rules for weaknesses:

Rule #1:

Just because you have a weakness does not mean you have to admit it. When you buy a car, the car salesman doesn't tell you that General Motors had 30 products recalled last year. He tells you that the car is excellent and you're getting a great price.

Regardless of how you feel about yourself, don't go on and on about your weaknesses. You have no moral or legal obligation to say anything negative about yourself, and it is your responsibility to say as many positive things about yourself as you can. This rule holds even if you were fired from your last job for incompetence and your previous boss told you that you were the worst employee on the planet.

Rule #2:

If you are forced to admit to a weakness, make sure it is a weakness of skill, not a character trait. Again, skills can be learned; character traits cannot. So, as an example, you could say something like, "Well, I have to admit I'd like to be better at using Excel. I just learned V-Lookup and Pivot Tables, but I want to learn more."

Rule #3:

Once you have admitted one of your skills is lacking, suggest your plan to improve that skill. Following on Rule #2, you could say, "However, I just enrolled in a weekend Advanced Excel course, and I'm looking forward to putting what I learn to work."

What are your career goals?

You could come up with short-term and long-term goals, whatever you choose, if not asked specifically. Your goals should involve achieving the company's vision and help it grow. But an entry-level person saying that he aims to become the company's CEO would sound too much. Be reasonable, and even if you aim big, your timing matters a lot.

Sample Answer

I want to excel in my field and then move within the company to learn about other departments and fields. Once I become a master in all, I would want to pursue my career in management as leadership comes naturally to me.

What is your biggest accomplishment?

One of the questions you will get in an interview at some point or another is to ask you to describe your most significant accomplishment.

For people early on in their career and who maybe don't have much job experience, the tendency may be to think about personal accomplishments.

Personal accomplishments are great, but business accomplishments are even better.   Think back over your work career and try and come up with something that made a difference to your employer. If you cannot, then try to come up with something that helped other people.

For example, if you ran a marathon and helped build a shelter for homeless people, mention the shelter for homeless people.

Just be careful to make sure your greatest accomplishment is not risky, such as skydiving or flying down a mountain in one of those squirrel suits.   Employers don't want employees whose off-hours activities might get them killed.

Why Did You or Are You Leaving Your Previous Employer?

Interviewers ask this question to find out if you were fired or left or are leaving your job. The rule here is simple.   If your last job was working for the worst company, with the worst boss and the worst group of coworkers on the planet, and you hated every minute of it.

The company was crooked, and the CEO went to jail; you will not mention any word to the interviewer. You will tell the interviewer that you are looking for the opportunity to take on more responsibilities, put more of your talents and abilities to work, and find an environment where you can make a meaningful contribution to the business's success.

Never speak disparagingly about a coworker, a subordinate, a supervisor, or a previous company. If you had a bad experience, evade the question and talk about the future opportunity you are looking for if pressed (which some interviewers will do), find something great to say about your former employer (even bad employers have some redeeming factors even if you must dig deep to find them).

If you were a student, it is also acceptable to say you left an employer to focus on your studies and complete a degree more in line with your career goals.

How well do you work under pressure?

Hopefully, this question will not make you feel too pressured as you answer it. Naturally, the answer would be yes, but aside from that, you also need to share a professional experience that you could handle well despite the pressure.

If the position itself involves a certain amount of pressure, you must highlight that you actually love working under pressure (but be honest about this as well, of course).

Sample answer:

I thrive in a fast-paced environment! I would much rather work under pressure than stay in a mundane job. I enjoy facing new challenges because it allows me to be dynamic and creative in what I do.
On the other hand, if the job is not that stressful, you must not give the interviewer the idea that you like pressure; otherwise, they might feel that the job will bore you.

Sample answer:

While I do not have any qualms about working under pressure, I enjoy a job where I can master specific skills and get into the details. I have always believed that quality should never be sacrificed for the sake of quantity.

Do you prefer to work on a team or lead the team instead?

Always handle such questions with care. If you are wondering why then switch places and think as an interviewer would think. Analyze the question now, and you will immediately see why this question needs special care.

If you are applying for a job that usually revolves around teamwork, it is a plus point that you prefer working as a team member, but staying limited to that would bar you from leadership roles. These are the roles performed by an individual who is leading the charge.

If you stick to the latter alone, you might not be a good fit at all. So how do you handle such a question? Fear not, as we shall look into various answers for this as well.

Sample Answer:

"I have been a team player throughout my professional life. I have worked on various teams and have learned how to operate matters fully. Through this experience, I was able to gain valuable lessons and learned how to lead teams as well.

In an ideal situation, a good team would have a good team leader and vice versa. But that is rarely the case. I have learned that to be an effective leader, you first need to work as a member of the team to fully understand matters and then lead the team once you have mastered the art."

These answers are more than justifiable and just about right in terms of length. If you needlessly stretch the answer, you might find yourself interrupted by the interviewer's next question. Speak briefly but with intent and purpose. Know what you need to convey and do so effectively.

Do you have any questions?

Identical questions to "Do you have any questions?"

•**Are you unclear about anything?**

Why does the interviewer ask this question?

The interviewer asks this question obviously to know if you are clear about everything talked about. So, if you have any doubts or questions, do not hesitate to discuss them with the interviewer.

This question could be thrown to you to see how different you are from the other candidate or how far you have researched the company.

A wrong answer to this question

"No, I am clear about everything."

What you need to know before answering this question

You should know that this question is a golden opportunity to satisfy your curiosity or find out more about the company, like the job position you applied for, the company, and the industry.   Ensure to avoid 'no' as an excellent answer to this question.

An excellent response to this type of question
Yes, I am a bit unclear about something. After a close examination of your interview questions, it seems you have a problem with returning your customers.

If I'm correct, can you please tell me a little more about the present situation and what would be required of the person that gets the job position?

Summary

Many fundamental questions are asked at virtually every interview. It is best to be prepared to answer all of them. Write them down in your journal. Practice delivering your interview in front of a mirror, or do a mock interview with a friend.

You need to prepare yourself as much as possible because the interviewer could ask you any question on the list, plus many more. Be prepared for both the expected and unexpected. There are always surprises, but you need to be ready to answer every question given to you to succeed in securing the position ultimately.

Chapter 3:

Expert
Preparation
for
Job Interviews

Knowing Yourself – First Step

The interview process is stressful, and one of the few times when you can feel completely in control of the interview flow is when you talk about yourself. This is something that is entirely in your control.

Often the degree of interview preparation marks the difference between the successful candidate and the unsuccessful candidate. While some of you might start the interview training process only after the job interview appointment is finalized, it is recommended that preparing for the interview starts right during your college days.

Most often, interviewers are amazed and amused at the sort of answers candidates provide to basic questions such as, 'Tell me about yourself.' Before you understand the prospective company, you should evaluate yourself and know what you are willing to offer the employer. Evaluate yourself in terms of your skills, educational qualifications, strengths and weaknesses, and career goals.

Remember that everyone seeking a job is a sort of salesperson. While the usual salesperson tries to sell his products, a candidate for a job interview has to sell his potential to the employer.

Since every employer almost always starts the interview process with this simple self-introduction type of question, you should make sure that you prepare for the same in advance. You might find it easier to prepare when you think of the job interview as a performance of sorts.

As with any performance, you should ensure that you have enough practice to carry it off well.

Make a list of your strengths and weaknesses; try to think of examples for each strength and weakness you are planning to quote. Try to list your achievements and interests – make sure at least a few of your interests are work-related.

You should not memorize all your lines and deliver them like an actor – it might not be natural, and it doesn't sound practical as well. They will come out as forced and will be less effective in an interview.

Moreover, if you forget what you were planning to say, you are sure to get distracted and lose confidence in yourself. However, it would be best to write down the answers to the questions you expect to ask during the interview.

Although you cannot be expected to judge yourself accurately, you should still try interviewing yourself at least a few times in front of the mirror. It is always advisable to record your performance so that you can judge yourself and your voice later. You will also be able to rectify any of your mistakes. Look at how you react to those moments when you are unsure about dealing with a question.

Take extra caution to analyze your pitch, tone, quality of voice, modulation, gestures, and clarity and make necessary alterations to suit those of the interviewer.

During the interview, it is natural that your nerves are all jagged, and your mind is on the verge of deep freeze, so now is the time to be aware of them and think of ways to control your fear and nervousness.

It is always suggested that you run a mental image of yourself and how you want to look on the interview day in your mind before you start your preparations.

Try participating in mock interview sessions or ask your trusted friends to simulate an interview session for you. Ask them to ask you typical interview questions and be very critical of your verbal and non-verbal communication.

Make sure that they are aware and offer critical opinions on your tone, appearance, body language, behavior, eye contact, and more. Be open to receive feedback and make the necessary corrections.

Self- Assessment for Better Performance

Self-assessment is a very important step in preparing for the interview, even though many are sometimes overlooked. It might be difficult to make the right career plans for your future, but you can start it by focusing on assessing yourself before jumping into the interview fray.

Self-assessment helps you recognize your strengths that you can emphasize during your interview. You can also identify your weaknesses that can be rectified and downplayed during the interview.

Self-assessment helps you build confidence in yourself. When you deeply delve into your background and history, you will be able to identify those strengths in you that can be contributed to your employer. When you understand your present skills and career goals, you will be able to answer interview questions better. Moreover, your answers might seem more natural and forthcoming.

When you undertake a self-assessment session, you are more likely to remember all your achievements and goals. You can use this information and connect it with your job profile and merge it with the company's requirements.

Once you have undertaken a self-assessment session, you will realize that it is a never-ending process. It not only helps you define your career goals but also makes it easier for you to have a deeper understanding of your skills, areas to improve, and your general attitude.

Self-assessment is a crucial part of job interview preparation; it helps you anticipate interviewer questions in advance and efficiently handle them.

Your self-assessment questions should include:

* Your qualifications that are related to the position
* Skills you can offer
* Examples from previous jobs
* Greatest accomplishments
* Motivating factors
* Positions interested in
* Expectations from the job

There are chances that you might find many of these questions to be too simple or easy to answer; however, you might find it easier discussing these questions with your friends but find it very uncomfortable discussing the same things with a recruiter.

One of the reasons why most of us have an uneasy feeling discussing topics with a recruiter is we all feel that we are being judged. While this might be partially true, you also must understand that there are no right or wrong answers to most questions.

Prep your Body Language

Body language plays a vital role in determining how you come across during the interview. When we communicate, non-verbal communication significantly impacts the listener more than we communicate through words. When we interact with others, we are continuously giving and receiving several non-verbal cues.

Non-verbal communication can play a significant role in personality assessment. It helps others learn a little more about you since most non-verbal messages you send play one of these five roles.

* They can agree to and repeat the message you have made.
* They can contradict the message you have made.
* They can underline a message you have made.
* They can add or improve on the verbal message.
* They can substitute a verbal message.

All non-verbal behaviors – from gestures, our mannerisms, the way we walk, talk, and stand, eye contact – everything tells a little more about us.

Although these quirks are natural to a person, we have to learn to keep these communication tools in control if we want to give a positive opinion about us. When you stop talking, it doesn't mean that you have stopped talking; in fact, you are continuously communicating non-verbally. Remember that non-verbal communication accounts for nearly 90% of all the messages you send to your listener.

Don't lean, don't slouch, sit straight: A bad posture can be deal-breaker, right then and there. Don't ever slouch; it suggests that the person is lazy. Leaning back is considered by many as being disinterested and arrogant, and leaning forward too much is regarded as a sign of arrogance.

According to many experts, you should aim for a neutral way to sit that is neither threatening nor lazy. Sit upright, slightly leaning to the front – may be at a 10 to 15-degree angle – towards the interviewer. This shows interest and attention. Sit as if there is a string suspended from the ceiling that is holding your head straight.

Hands communicate too: Most of us are unsure what to do with our hands during our interview or addressing a crowd. Our hands do a lot of communication on their own, and they can be quite a distractive thing during the interview.

You should be able to find a way in which your hands don't come in the way of your interview and yourself. You should note that the minute you start pointing at the interviewer to make a point or bang the table in aggression, you are not taking your case anywhere.

Let your hands rest loosely on your lap or the table in front of you. If you don't soon find a place for your hands, you are more likely to see them planting themselves nervously in your pockets, fiddling with your hair, scratching your nose, touching your face.

Fiddling with your hair, neck, or face is considered a sign of uncertainty and dishonesty. Several body language experts agree that touching your nose or lips signals that the person is lying.

Crossed arms or hanging by your sides? This is a question asked by many candidates unsure of how to manage their arms – is it better to cross your arms, hang them by your sides or hold them behind your back?

Crossing arms against your chest suggests that you are aggressive or resist change. It signals that you are not open to change and are not flexible. Folding arms against your chest also shows that you are defensive and are feeling threatened. Holding your arms behind your back is not a natural position as it inhibits the free movement of your arms. It makes you appear stiff.

Beware of your feet:

The way you rest your feet also tells a lot about you. When you cross your legs or rest them easily on the floor suggests that you are confident about yourself.

Constantly jiggling your feet or moving your legs around too much indicates nervousness; it can also distract the interviewer. If you rest your ankle on your knee, you signal that you are arrogant and trying too much to look cool. If you cross your legs too high, you appear defensive.

Eyes tell a thousand tales:

Your eyes indeed speak a thousand stories that your mouth might not reveal. One of the first cues that you give about yourself through non-verbal communication is through your eyes.

Maintain eye contact throughout the interview session; however, don't try to stare down the interviewer. While it is important to look confident and look at the interviewer in the eye, you really shouldn't continually stare at them.

Break away the eye contact now and then. Looking at someone for extended periods makes you look aggressive and creepy – you don't want to give that image. Imagine being the interviewer, and you are looking all over the place.

As an interviewer, you will find it difficult to concentrate on the answers provided by the interviewee. You might not believe the answers either.

When you maintain eye contact with the interviewer, you signal that you are attentive and interested in what the interviewer is saying. When you keep darting your eyes from one place to another, you signal that you are dishonest.

When you constantly seem distracted or keep moving your eyes upward, you are either lying or trying to be sure of something that you are not. Continually looking down indicates that you are not confident in yourself.

To nod or not to nod: How much nodding is too much? Nod once or twice when the interviewer is making a solid point you agree with. After that, you have to find a center position, hold your head still and stay still.

Nodding constantly like a bubble-headed doll is irritating and distracting. Keep your nodding to a bare minimum - at least for the sake of the interviewer!

Dress up for the interview

Everyone gets only one chance to make the first impression. If you dress the part, you are more likely to convince the interviewers that you are perfect for your job.

The way you dress and carry yourself says a lot about your character and how you might behave if they employed you. If you want to impress the interviewers and get the job, you should be willing to take some time out to get the right dress and accessories.

Bad hygiene is a deal-breaker:

Being clean will undoubtedly take you places. Regardless of whether you will attend an interview or go out with a couple of friends, it would help if you remembered that bad hygiene could ruin even the world's most expensive clothes.

A fresh body and a fresh mind will help you face the interview panel quickly. Wash your hands before you attend the interview, especially if you have sweaty and sticky hands. Since you would normally shake at least a few hands, you should make sure that your hands smell and feel nice.

Look and Smell nice: Looking and smelling nice is going to help you feel confident about yourself. While it might be essential to smell nice, you should not overwhelm the interviewer with fragrance too strong. Your face is the first thing your interviewers will notice, so make sure it looks fresh, approachable, and professional.

A smile is the best makeup you can wear. Make sure that your eye makeup is just enough to accentuate your lashes. A subtle lip shade is perfect, as you don't want to be looking tacky.

You might have the best and most colorful collection of eye shadows, but this is not exactly the right time to show your collection or your makeup prowess. Keep the reds, blues, and greens safely tucked in your house, and try to look like you will work and not to a club!

Groom yourself:

Pay attention to your hair, as you have to present yourself professionally to the interview panel. Your hair should not be too dry that it looks like natural hay or too greasy that it sticks to the sides of your head like wet paper.

Color your hair if you feel you have to, but avoid bright colors that look like you have lost a bet with your hairdresser. Avoid bright-colored hair clips and avoid spiking your hair; ensure your hair doesn't distract the interviewer's attention.

Check your fingernails before entering the interview room. You should have job-ready fingernails at all times. Your prospective employers are likely to notice your fingernails when you extend your hand for your very first handshake.

Try to avoid too bright nail colors; always keep your nails short or keep them even. If you have the habit of biting your nails, try to cut your nails short before the interview and resist the temptation of biting your nails while waiting for your turn at the interview.

Dress to look the part:

If the interview you are attending is for a career in a professional environment, you should try to look your part. There are certain rules and regulations for presenting yourself in an interview. If you have dressed up poorly or in a too casual manner, you are sure to stick out from the rest like an odd person out.

Check out the company's culture; if the employees in the company wear casuals every day, it is alright if you attend the interview casually.

Men:

You should dress in a manner that is appropriate to the position applied to. You should not dress up for the job; you should dress down. If you are unsure about the dress code suitable for the interview, it is better to go conservative.

Men are better off wearing a dark-colored, long-sleeved suits. Formal shoes are a must; they help complete the look. A dark-colored suit with a light-colored shirt, color-coordinated socks, and a neat tie is perfect for the job interview.

Wear something you are comfortable in, not necessarily what you look good in. You are better off buying a new suit if all you have is something you wore on your 15th birthday!

Don't wear loud colors; anything bright and flashy should be avoided entirely. Your clothes should be neatly washed and pressed.

Women:

A suit with a skirt is the right choice for you if you want a formal dress for the interview. A dark-colored skirt and a color-coordinated blouse is a better choice than a mismatched dress.

For a business casual look, you can try wearing a cardigan or a sweater as well. More importantly, make sure you don't wear see-through clothes that might divert your interviewer's attention to somewhere you don't want.

Wear something that you are comfortable in – it need not be the latest to hit the fashion scene. The skirt should be of a decent and comfortable height so that you don't have to keep pulling it down during the interview.

Shoes can make or mar an interview; make sure you have the right ones for the interview. They should be comfortable to wear, gel well with your clothes, and have one solid color – preferably in black. Make sure that the shoes have reasonably high heels – not too high to hurt your feet and not too low to make you look like you are shuffling around in flip flops. Check that your heels do not have anything sticking to them.

Accessorize Yourself: Unlike what you have heard about accessories, they are a crucial part of your attire. Wear tasteful, subtle jewelry. No flashy jewelry or anything that might set you off like a Bobo, the Clown! Anything stylish and elegant like a watch or a scarf that accentuates your costume will do you wonders. A sleek bag or a wallet will do well too.

Know the Company

Researching about the employers is the first chance you get to show your skills as a prospective recruit. Find out as much as you can about the organization, its goals, present market share, services, organizational structure, and recent achievements.

You should learn more about the job you are applying to. Understand the job requirements, and try to match them with your educational qualification and experience. When you know about the employer, you will be better prepared to sync and shape your answers to line up your skills to the organizational requirements.

You should know about the job processes of the company so that you can talk convincingly about how you will be able to fit into their work culture. The best place where you can find authentic information about the company is their official website.

Their 'about us' page and social media pages will provide information about their products, services, and offers. In addition to knowing what they do, you should also know why they are into this business. If they ask you questions about, 'where do you see yourself in the near future,' you will answer it better if you know where the company is going.

You should also know the company's culture, office atmosphere, and dress code if you want to fit into their mold easily. This also helps you dress accordingly as you might stick out like a sore thumb if you come dressed in a three-piece suit and the interviewer is dressed in casuals.
Similarly, you should get to know the company's current events, any new projects they have undertaken, new deals they have signed with other organizations. You should know a little about the organization's CEO, organizational plans, and goals.

Knowing the company will help you answer their questions properly without taking a wild guess. Moreover, you will also be better equipped to ask them educated, clear, and relevant questions without embarrassing yourself.

Know the Job Description and Job Requirements
Asking the right questions is as important as giving the right answers.

It would be best if you asked yourself some questions about the job before preparing for the interview. Know about the job, its requirements in terms of skill, education, experience, and training.

Even if the job description is put up on the company website, it is better to understand it clearly from the HR Manager or job consultant. With the latest job description in hand, you will be better equipped to sync the requirements with your key skills.

Before attending the interview, you should know the person who will interview you and learn a little about them. The best way to do this is to check out their LinkedIn and Facebook profiles.

Summary

It is vital to see that appearance is very important regarding interviews. You have to look and smell your best when you go into this process.

First impressions are crucial, so you want everyone to like you at first glance. Otherwise, you can easily spoil the interview and leave a bitter aftertaste in the interviewer's mouth.

It is important to take care of your appearance. Otherwise, you'll look like a slob who probably shouldn't have been invited to the interview. Dress to impress. Take that extra hour to do your hair.

Wash yourself thoroughly. Avoid smoking beforehand. Freshen your breath. Do all things effectively. You will see that you can make a strong impression and be able to succeed in the interview.

Chapter 4:

Interview Tips to Close the Deal and get Hired

Thanking the Interviewer

There is no excuse for not thanking the interviewer. You should ask for the interviewers' business cards and send them a letter of appreciation as early as possible. Since we are in the email era, you can shoot the thank you letter as soon as you can find the time. If you think that the company will recruit very quickly, you should send your appreciation letter as early as possible before they decide.

Proper communication will be appreciated, and make sure you make use of the thank you letter. Ensure that the thank you letter is more than just a simple thank you note. Convey to the interviewer your interest in the position and the company.

Pick a topic that you discussed during the interview so that the interviewer knows who you are. Review some of the points discussed during the interview so that their memory is refreshed. You can also reiterate some of the skills and educational qualifications you possess. You can also talk about any significant qualities in you that you missed mentioning during the personal interview. If you receive an immediate reply, you can be sure that they are interested in you.

Follow-up Communication

Follow-up communication is necessary as it shows your interest in the job and the organization. It is always essential that you reply immediately to any of the emails sent by the organization's representatives. Any delay in communication would be considered as sheer lethargy or disinterest.

Make sure that you get the business cards of your recruiter and send the proper thank you note. Take care to use not only the right tone but also the correct grammar and spelling. Take extra caution to get the name and spelling of the interviewer right.

Before leaving the interview location, enquire the right persons about the next steps in the selection process. In some cases, the interviewer would spell out the steps in the selection process. If, in case, you don't receive any information, make sure you ask for it.

If the interviewer asks you to call back on Thursday, you better call up on Thursday. Not a day early and certainly not a day late. Failure to call on the stipulated day could prove detrimental to your candidacy.

There is nothing wrong with being a little persistent. While some of you might assume that being persistent might make you look desperate, the fact is, recruiters appreciate a bit of persistence. Being persistent doesn't mean you have to keep badgering the recruiter. Decide on the right technique and the right amount of aggressiveness, depending on the position you are looking for.

Accepting the Offer Letter

Once the company has given you a formal letter of offer, you can either accept it or deny it. However, regardless of your acceptance or denial, you should ensure that you intimate the company in writing.

When you accept the offer letter, it is always better to write a formal letter of acceptance to confirm to the details provided in the offer letter. Before accepting, make sure you read the letter at least a couple of times. You have to be sure about the details of employment provided in the offer letter.

Before sending in the acceptance letter, it is always better to acknowledge the offer over the phone. Call the hiring manager and let them know about your intentions to accept the offer.

Once you have confirmed your intentions over the phone, it is time to write a formal letter of acceptance. Make sure that the letter is brief and concise.

Don't start rambling about your virtues; it is time to keep it simple. Your offer letter should contain a formal note of thanks for selecting you, and appreciate the opportunity provided to you. Mention the details of employment such as salary, benefits, designation, probation periods, and more.

Confirm the date of joining; it is better not to leave it ambiguous. You can use this opportunity to clarify the doubts you might have had and inform the company if you cannot join them on the specified day because of any prior engagement.

Handling Rejection with Grace

Candidates often look at rejection as a disgrace. Being rejected after performing well in a job interview can severely dent a person's confidence.

However, since you know that you have given your best, there is certainly nothing wrong with you, but your skills do not match the company's needs. By thinking objectively, you can certainly look at rejection as a learning process.

You should have learned something from the interview; you should have understood your skills better. The first and foremost step is self-assessment – identifying your competencies, strengths and weaknesses.

If you have been rejected just this one time, you can certainly look at rejection as a step towards better employment opportunities. However, if you have been rejected more than a couple of times, you should look at where you go wrong, understand your body language, and plan your next steps.

The next step in dealing with rejection is addressing the issues. One of the most common reasons for rejection is the lack of technical knowledge.

The reason for being rejected by one company can be turned around to become the main reason for getting accepted by another company.

Remember that rejection is undoubtedly not feedback and should not be perceived as one.

Never carry the interview rejection baggage around. You have to approach each new job with a fresh mind and perspective.

It would be best if you started working on tailoring your resume to meet the new needs of the next interview.

Learn from the mistakes you made in your last interview since each company and each recruiter will have a different approach towards interviewing and different ideas about an ideal candidate.

All you have to do is keep learning from your mistakes and developing your skills and talents to meet the changing needs of the job market.

CHAPTER 5:

Job Interview Resources

Job Search Engines (JSE)

Now that we have discussed skillsets and what employers may be seeking in employees let's discuss how you can find the work you want.

Unlike the classified section of many beloved Sunday newspapers, today's job market can be researched via the Internet through job search engines. These "engines" or websites are a necessary component to searching for work in various industries.

Since there are many choices in using job search engines, I will reference the ones that have worked for me, including Craigslist, Monster, CareerBuilder, and Indeed.

Craigslist

Craigslist.com (search for the craigslist site specific to your area). More than any other site, this site has linked me to some unique and ongoing projects. You will have to create an account to begin your job search.

A proven method in my job search activities has been searching those city links where I know there may be more qualified work for me than others. This could be Boston, New York, Chicago, or San Francisco. Those cities where writing, publishing, and creative projects are prevalent.

Learn to weed out the actual jobs from falsely advertised ones. Learning how to "trawl" or to seek and know how to spot ads that may be fraudulent or not forthcoming was a learning curve I was happy to go through. Make certain as you choose a job search engine that works for you, you learn to spot them, too.

Fraudulent ads usually have these characteristics:

* If you find a similar context in the ads under a different city search

* An ad that asks for money to allow you to resource their list of clients

* An ad that will not pay you for copious amounts of work as an "intern"

* The spelling is atrocious, and the grammar is not at all in keeping with the English language

Today, I maintain several top-notch clients I have cultivated on Craigslist and am proud to be working with them.

Monster

As a career search engine and job board, monster.com offers job searches and articles with tried and true information on the trends in navigating the expanding virtual global workforce at any age. Using this website as a job search engine, you will have to create an account and upload your resume to be active for employers to search for you.

Then, you can very easily look for employment in your field by searching the jobs database. The system has been improved for straightforward navigation with abundant tips, leads, and job search-related articles.

Monster covers the gamut for employees of every age and talent group, from remaining relevant as we age in the workforce to knowing what questions might be illegal if they are asked during a job interview.

Monster also offers a modest yet free assessment of your resume at no cost. However, be prepared to be linked to resume writers associated with Monster, should you continue to click through their overview of services in this area.

CareerBuilder

According to bloggers at Undercover Recruiter, careerbuilder.com is on a par with other job search engines. Yet, most of the job applicants on CareerBuilder hold college degrees from online or accredited schools.

Indeed and Monster offer job opportunities to teenagers, first-time high-schoolers, students still in high school, or first-time college graduates.

CareerBuilder does not cater to these job seekers. Even if you haven't yet graduated with a college degree, consider what you might have in terms of skills you have already gained.

What you have studied to date can sometimes be utilized as information in your job search, especially if you have strong technology and administrative skills.

If this is the case, seek employers who may assist you in completing your education or training so that your career trajectory is constantly moving upward.

Indeed

Considered the most inclusive job board, indeed.com includes work at home, seasonal jobs, contract positions, and volunteer opportunities.

Indeed allows job seekers and employers to filter and manage applications. Companies seeking a high turnaround rate for employees are likely to post on this service. It is a fairly easy-to-use platform.

Samuel Edwards, a writer for Inc. Magazine online, stated that Indeed, as a job search engine, helps to streamline the searching process since it is an all-inclusive site without one having to visit other sites for related opportunities. The search results go directly into your email box if you are set up for this function.

As a no-frills JSE, it does what it is set up to do - deliver leads that are programmed for your area of expertise.

Common Mistakes Made During An Interview

Having inappropriate or questionable content on social networking sites.

Remember, organizations do a background check before recruiting anyone. About 70% of managers in the recruiting department of different organizations have said that candidates make a grave mistake of uploading and posting compromising content in various social networking sites.

Through the content, managers get to learn about writing skills and other insights of candidates.

Asking few questions

This portrays that the concerning person is not interested in the job. The key is to ask not vital but smart questions. This way, you will not come across as a clueless or disinterested person.

Being overconfident

The younger generation mostly makes this. They are conditioned and trained to have a strong sense of self-esteem, which develops as overconfidence. They often make the interview process only about them.

Turning Up Late

This should not happen in the first place, so you don't need to take the chance. Set off very early. Its irritating how traffic and everything else seems to work against you only on the day of your interview.

If it happens, you had better have such a reasonable excuse that it cannot be ignored. And at every opportunity, call in and let the interviewer know.

Fidgeting with Unnecessary Props

Please! Please! Please! Find a very diplomatic way of hiding your nerves and fears. Don't fidget with the pen, the books, folders, mobile phone, nails, your thigh or beard - don't do it. It sends too many wrong messages.

For example, you may be lying about something, or that you are not confident you can settle in the role, etc.

Unclear Answering and Rambling

If you don't know the answer to a question, say so with a "sorry," but don't rant something totally off track. It isn't the time to fool your way out. It can make the interviewer feel their intelligence is being insulted. And don't mumble. If the interviewer(s) has to ask what you just said more than three times, then you will start to lose it all on their score-sheet.

Speaking Negatively About Your Current Employer

If you don't have anything good to say about your former employer(s), please don't say anything. It won't go well for you if you do. The potential employer is likely to see himself in the same position when you finally leave their employment.

Discussing Money or Time Off

Unless it is put on the table by the interviewer, avoid as far as possible talking about salary packages, sick and holiday leave, or welfare policies. It soon becomes obvious you are not attending the interview for anything other than for money, and people with that kind of dispensation hardly add any value to any role – they take!

Not Following Up

Not many candidates do this after an interview, so the few who do it get an extra advantage. Even if you think your performance at the interview wasn't that great, you should still send the potential employer a short email message to thank you for the opportunity.

You are still very enthusiastic about getting the job. Don't leave it days after the interview – do it the same day of the interview. The little extra effort only shows that you are a cut more serious about the role than others.

Assuming an Interview is an Interrogation

Too many interviewees assume that an interview is a process of asking a series of questions and finding responses to those questions. This is simply not the case. An interview is a two-way process.

The employer is as much on trial in an interview as the interviewee. Be prepared to probe the interviewer for information and follow-up questions until you are satisfied with your answers.

Remember - this is your career that we're talking about! You don't want to wind up at a company that files for bankruptcy six months after you join; the signs of their impending doom have been painfully obvious to see had you just been a bit more assertive in your line of questioning.

Responding to a question without thinking

Sometimes in an interview, we can lose focus. When this happens we either lose track of what we are saying or don't know how to respond to a question. In this instance, the worst thing to do is to panic and blurt out the first thing that comes to mind.

If you find yourself in this situation, choose a more constructive approach. Win yourself some time by repeating the question aloud to help you refocus or ask the interviewer to repeat it.

If you've forgotten what you are saying, admit as much to the interviewer and ask him/her to repeat the question. Never try to muddle through without focusing on a question, as it will only confuse you and the interviewer.

Not doing your pre-interview homework

If you fail to make time to do your research on the employer, plan how to emphasize the qualities on your resume, or what questions you should ask the employer when prompted, you'll be doing yourself a huge injustice. The better prepared you are to answer questions about yourself, your career, and your personality, the more likely you will impress the interviewer and land that job.

Being Arrogant

Knowing that you have answers to all the questions being asked and being happy with it should not make you arrogant. Don't start speaking or behaving as you've already got the job – you might be unpleasantly surprised. It will be far more profitable to your chances if you keep calm throughout the interview. If you know something that a panelist or interviewer doesn't know, control yourself. Don't let it show on the large screen of your ego.

Nothing puts off a potential employer than an arrogant candidate – from the point it is first exhibited, most interviewers simply shut down from listening to you any further.

Turning the Weakness Question into A Positive
When interviewers ask about your weaknesses, they know we all have a few, so it's pretty insulting to their intelligence if you try to paint yourself as someone without any. Instead, I suggest thinking about a weakness that can be improved but which does not impact any of the core requirements of the job you are applying for.

Get caught lying.

A definite guarantee that you will not get the job is to lie during the job interview. If you are going to make a bold claim or state something that is not true, seriously think about your chances of getting away with it. Companies run background checks on potential hires. Whether it is about your credentials, accomplishments, or work history, honesty will usually be the best policy.

It's tempting, I know, but honestly, what would it prove? If you lie about qualifications, the employer will find out. If you lie about your career history, the employer will find out. If you lie about your knowledge and experience, you could get into a very embarrassing situation in the interview itself!

Inappropriate humor.

Be confident, but avoid cracking jokes unnecessarily or saying things probably best left unsaid. A little touch of humor could work in your favor, provided that it is appropriate to the interview context. You do not need to be funny, especially when it is at the expense of appropriateness and formality. The last thing you want is the hiring manager to think you are not serious about the job opportunity.

Getting personal.

A job interview is a formal meeting to assess if you are the right fit for a job. Everything in your personal life, subjective opinions, and feelings should be left outside the door and not be brought up during the interview.

Bad-mouthing previous companies

It does not reflect well on you to talk negatively about companies on your resume. It's natural to have a few bad experiences but be sure to paint them in the right light. If you talk negatively about a previous company, it implies that you will speak negatively about the company you're interviewing for now in the future. I've seen CEO's reject candidates at the last minute because of this.

Don't come under-dressed

This is a sensitive one. It's hard to know exactly what to wear. Overdressing typically means wearing a suit. Use your judgment, of course, but always lean toward overdressing. 75% of interviewers have said that most candidates turn up dressed shabbily or inappropriately for an interview. Follow the above attire checklist for creating a great impression.

Cursing

Please watch your language. Cursing implies that you don't communicate professionally in the workplace.

Summary

It is always wise to thank your interviewer, and this chapter has outlined different ways you can go about it. The chapter has also taught you how to follow up, accept a job offer or embrace rejection with grace. Interview etiquette is vital. Avoid making common mistakes discussed in this chapter.

Conclusion

I hope you have found the tips and suggestions gathered in this book helpful for preparing for your job interview. Hopefully, you will now have a better idea of things to do and not to do to ace that job interview. Using the information in this book will undoubtedly improve your interview skills for the better, no doubt about it!

The best thing, psychologically, to know going into an interview is that a company has already approved of you on paper. They already know you know to successfully do the job or else they wouldn't be wasting everyone's time.

Time is money, so bringing you into the company already costs them money regardless of how long the interview process is. Companies don't just throw money around. Having you in there does mean something special.

Going to interviews can be a brutally stressful process, especially in high-demand industries. When you arrive at an interview and see a line of people or meet people who are just coming out, it can stir up some extreme levels of competitiveness in us or a sense of instant defeat. Honestly, the best mentality to take into this situation is that it's a competition.

Preparation for a stressful experience is the key to success. It's evident to an interviewer how prepared a candidate is after the first few questions, possibly even the first question.

Some people may be masters in their industry but are terrible people to work with. More often than not, the guy with the relatable personality and mediocre skillset will get the job over the exceptionally talented jerk. Know who you will be working for, prepare for oddball questions with deeper meanings and be enthusiastic, and you got this.

Practice makes perfect! As with doing anything, you have to put in the time and effort to practice the art of interviewing either into the mirror with yourself or to your friends and family members. Be brutally honest with yourself because this is the time when you can make mistakes and still stand a chance to get that job. A few weeks before going to the interview, you will want to research what the company is about and the sort of questions you might get asked. Keep practicing, and you will appear naturally confident on the big day.

You also have to understand that not every interview is going to result in a job offer. Yes, you will fail (unless you are REALLY skillful), and that is okay!

As long as you have presented your most authentic and capable self, you have done your best. Learn from your mistakes and write them down in the following interview. Don't sit around and keep saying you wanted to start something, do this, do that, go ahead and do it now. Later is never a better time to do something. Get started today, kick some butt and show everyone how awesome you are. Be yourself, keep hunting, and good luck!

YOU GOT THIS!

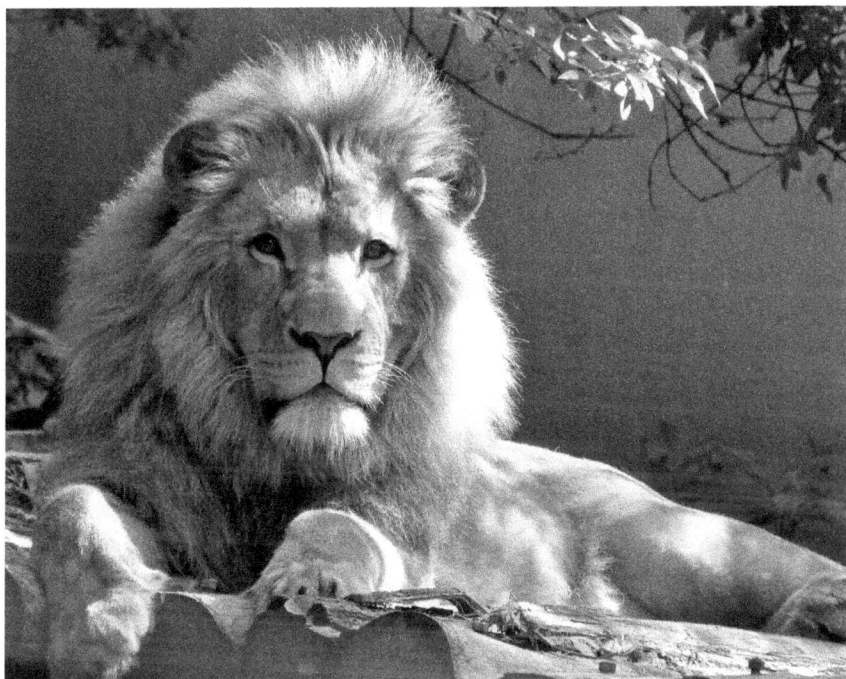

Finally, if you enjoyed this book, please take the time to share your thoughts and post a review on Amazon. It'd be greatly appreciated!

Many Thanks,

Brian Mahoney

**Job Interview Prep Book for Men, Women and Teens
Answer the Tough Questions and handle Your
Interview with Confidence and Ease**

We want to thank you for the purchase of this book
and more importantly, thank you for reading it to the
end. We hope your reading experience was
pleasurable and that you would inform your family
and friends on Facebook, Twitter or other social
media.

We would like to continue to provide you with high-
quality books, and that end, would you mind leaving
us a review on Amazon.com?

Just use the link below, scroll down about 3/4 of the
page and you will see images similar to the one
below.

We are extremely grateful for your assistance.
Warm Regards, MahoneyProducts Publishing

Book Link:

Customer reviews
4.6 out of 5   4.6 out of 5
stars   6 global ratings

5 star   64%_
4 star   36%-
3 star 0% (0%)   0%
2 star 0% (0%)   0%
1 star 0% (0%)

Review this product
Share your thoughts with other customers
(Write a Customer Review)

How To Get
Money for
Small Business
Start Up

How to Get Massive Money from
Crowdfunding, Government Grants
and Government Loans

Ramsey Colwell

You might also enjoy:

How To Get Money for Small Business Start Up:

How to Get Massive Money from Crowdfunding, Government Grants and Government Loans

Imagine you can have the knowledge you want to start your business and live the Hassle Free All-American Lifestyle of Independence, Prosperity and Peace of Mind. Discover...

* How to apply for a grant to start a small business (over 2,432 government programs are available!)

* How to apply for a small business startup loan (There is up to $5 Million Dollars waiting for you!)

* I answer the question "How do I start a small business" ...with quick & easy step by step instructions.

* How to Get Free Colossal Cash from Crowd Funding

* How to reach a Billion people for free with Video Marketing!

* Step by step instructions for writing an Amazing Business Plan

Money is there for the taking! So Don't wait... You'll wait your life away...

Amazon.com Book Link:

https://www.amazon.com/dp/1951929144

www.ingramcontent.com/pod-product-compliance
Lightning Source LLC
Chambersburg PA
CBHW071510210326
41597CB00018B/2710